Nirvana

By

A A Prideaux

A CIP catalogue record for this title is

Available from the British Library.

ISBN 978-0-9930676-6-2

www.paganuspublishing.co.uk

First published in 2015

Paganus Publishing

Ruthin

Wales

Paganus Publishing

I am dedicating this book to my other self...

Nirvana is the stillness of mind we all possess once we remove the delusional emotions of the sensory world.

A A Prideaux

Contents

FOREWORD

I initially began to write a longer project about a method you should apply, in order to learn how to control your life, but I changed my mind partway through.

There was a reason for that. I wanted you to use the information given in this book and prove the method to yourself. If I give you examples, or argue and debate each point, it will distract from the information I want you to use every day for the rest of your life.

You can begin in this very moment. You do not have to ask anyone's permission and no one needs to know what you are doing. You can practice while in a crowd of people and keep a smile on your face. All the while, you will be improving your health, your mind and your circumstances. One day, those same people will wonder about the sudden change which has taken place in your life. But, you will know that it was not so sudden and you brought about the change yourself.

Many of us are confused or sad or broke. There seems no reason why one person succeeds and another does not, even though they began in the same place. Once you have learned this process, you will understand why. And you will never look at your life in the same way again.

I want you to learn quickly and I hope I pass the information on succinctly. This book needs to be short enough for you to read easily, because you will be going back to it time and time again. Repetition and practice are going to be your helpers.

This will be a serious scientific experiment if you choose to undertake it. It cannot do you harm. Follow the instructions, start slowly and with awareness and prove it to yourself. That is always the best proof. Listening to other peoples' experiences tend to separate you from your own experience. Otherwise you will always try and compare their experience to your own.

I am not asking you to believe me. I am asking you to read the book, understand the instructions and put them into practice. Then see what happens.

HOW WE CREATE OUR OWN LIFE

The first point you must recognise and accept, is that the whole world is composed of your own thoughts objectified through your consciousness. The whole world.

How you experience every single one of your day to day events is down to the fact you are creating the experience in your mind. All the bad luck, the horror, the enemies, the irritating boss, the illness, the fat, the debt. I could go on. All of it, you create in your mind.

It is such a depressing thought, when you think about it coldly. To learn that everything you have been thinking about, has brought all of your problems to your door. What a crock. That doesn't make any sense at all. We all know that it is really the fault of the government, our parents, our boss and the secret society of lizards that run the world...

Or perhaps not, perhaps it is you.

The basis of what you will be learning in this book, is how to become aware of your thoughts and feelings. Because those are what have been creating your life to date and will be from today onwards. It may mean nothing to you now, because you cannot remember thinking anything which has resulted in the effects you are currently experiencing. But you have you know and eventually you will come to realise this fact for yourself. Then you will know exactly how to think and feel in order that you may have a great life. The life you want.

Your consciousness has been conditioned by your reactions to all of the experiences you have experienced during your lifetime .As a result of this conditioning, you continue to experience a life you believe is real and separate to you. But it isn't. Test yourself right now and ask whether you consider the world and all of it's sensory objectifications to be separate to you. You have failed the test if you think so. Everything is in you. Your consciousness is not only the cause of your world, but also forms the constituent parts of it.

You need to understand what consciousness is, before you can understand the first step to building your ideal, happy and healthy life.

You may have heard of the subconscious and the conscious minds. For this teaching, you need to understand that these minds are the same minds which work in harmony with each other. And in order to use your consciousness to the best result, you must study the relationship between the two minds.

The conscious mind is subjective and discriminatory and the sub conscious is objective and non-discriminatory. The conscious is effect and the subconscious cause. It is important for you to recognise that.

You use your conscious to have an idea and you then impress that idea on to your subconscious. Your subconscious then proceeds to work out ways to produce the idea in your world experience. Most people perform this action unconsciously and so the subconscious uses our established memories and habits in order to complete the unconsciously requested action. The subconscious accepts whatever idea you impress upon it, without question and cares nothing about your motivation. When done with feeling, the subconscious magnifies and accelerates the manifestation in size and speed. You only have to look at what you are producing in your life to discover what feelings and emotions you are using at the moment and causing these effects.

Once you begin to comprehend the nature of creation, then you begin to see how you must learn to control your ideas and feelings. You must learn how to do these acts with awareness. The sloppy attitude to the way you have been thinking your life to date, has been the cause of your problems. You have recognised no correlation between your thoughts and feelings and the occurrences in your life. And you should. You have to begin recognising what is really going on.

This is all excellent news. Because once you understand what I am telling you and it shouldn't take you too long if you maintain an open mind, you can lay out the best possible life for yourself. You can dream big, bigger than you ever have before. You no longer need to pay attention to any of the so called facts or the reasons in the sensory world. You don't need to change any of them. For they are only the effects of an idea you impressed upon your subconscious and it dutifully expressed the same in your world experience. Your world has no life of it's own other than the life you are giving it. If you want to change your life, you only need to impress another idea onto your subconscious with as much feeling as you can muster. Use faithful intention rather than force. You will soon get the knack.

You may need to do this several times a day for several weeks. Maybe it takes only once. The time it takes is dependent upon the strength of your belief and the feeling you put into the granted wish you want to manifest. For nothing exists outside of your mind. You have to believe in yourself and have faith in the power of creation you have right now, within you.

Your sub conscious accepts everything you tell it and accepts it strongly through your feelings. It will then set about creating your wish for you. Think about the times you felt as though there was one case of bad luck after another, befalling you. You thought that the first act of bad luck arrived randomly and then believed that randomness was it's cause. You then gave your subconscious the false information that you were not capable of sorting out all that had randomly appeared. This negative reaction of yours began a helpless series of events which manifested in your life. Or perhaps one day you felt ill and quickly felt worse and worse. So you took some medicine, or saw a specialist and accepted whatever it was they said. You took on board this prophecy from someone you believe knows more than you, for good or ill and followed the path of illness which they gave to you. And the more scared you became, the more insistent was your negative reaction to your problem. Your subconscious dutifully objectified your instruction and accepted your negative prognosis. And all the time, it was you who had created the original instruction. Perhaps you were mentally running away from another problem that you had also created. But you forgot about that. This is why it will be important to watch your thoughts and feelings from now on. Note your thoughts and feelings prior to the effects. You have been taught that the cause of your misfortune is separate to you. Your subconscious will accept any idea you give it as a fact which lives within itself and will respond exactly to that instruction.

Once you understand this, you begin your trip to total freedom.

What you must now do is think of your favourite idea and impress it upon your subconscious. You maintain the feeling of the idea having been completed which will encourage your subconscious to mirror your idea. Then it will materialise in your life.

You are not learning a way of magically producing your wishes. You are doing this unconsciously all the time and have been doing so, since time immemorial. Now, I am teaching you how to do it quickly and with complete awareness. This way you will begin to get the results you want, for a change.

You must learn to remain aware for most of the time and use the motive power of feeling to assist your subconscious to carry out your wishes. It cares nothing about good or bad, but merely carries out your wishes unquestioningly. You can desire the most hideous experiences and have them manifested for eternity. But, really, why would that be your choice? Why would you choose to watch and live in the worst film you have ever seen?

Spend some time thinking about what it is that you want to have and want to be. Then you can be sure about what it is that you want to create. You must believe that you have already received what you want, in order that the feeling can be mirrored in your life. You must feel and believe that you are surrounded by the consequences of your wish. Your wishes live in the state of mind and mood which matches perfectly. For example, plenty of money might mean security and calmness.

Breathe in that mood, walk in that mood and sleep in that mood. It is more than important to feel that your idea has been achieved. It is this feeling that will carry the manifestation forward. The longer you can calmly keep this feeling going, the quicker the manifestation will become a natural part of you and your life. The idea cannot be manifested until it is felt, but once it is felt, it must be manifested. When you have manifested situations or possessions that you now find you no longer want, then an opposing feeling must be conjured within your conscious mind and body and a new idea and mood impressed upon your subconscious. This must bring this new point of view into force

It is absolutely pointless to try and change the previously imagined situation. It merely hangs in front of you as a hologram would. Do not try and shut it down or change it. Conjure up something new and then work and feel with that. If you do not control and discipline your feelings, you will conjure up experiences which are not desirable. It is only once constant discipline is practised, that your experiences become the ones you truly desire. You could think and feel right now, right this second, 'Everything that happens in my life is wonderful and beautiful and I am happy and healthy.' Or whatever your wish is.

It is essential that you do not entertain in any way, the thoughts and feelings about anything which opposes your true desires. You must never think or talk about anyone in a negative way, nor wish them ill. Never dwell on your own shortcomings, either physical or material, because you will be forcing your own subconscious to accept these thoughts as limitations to any outcome it may be creating. These shortcomings will be brought into the story that your subconscious is weaving for you. You don't want that.

There is absolutely no judgement for anything you say or do. Your subconscious is non-judgmental. This limitation you are insisting be brought into your life, is what is preventing you from moving into the area you want to live, or the job you want to have.. Karma is only the effects you are reaping in your own life because of the causes you are planting. There is no outside judge determining to bring you a fate similar to the one you chose to inflict on someone else.

You are reaping objectively what you sow subjectively.

Do not hope that a certain thing may not happen to you. Only imagine that the opposite has already happened to you, such as, 'I have the job.'

Your subconscious will create whatever it is you are instructing it to produce. You do not have to think of the road to your dream. Merely imagine what it would feel like to arrive and impress your subconscious with that feeling. It will not let you down. It cannot.

Every feeling you have, makes an impression which must be expressed in a physical form, whether good or bad. To counteract this, you must immediately put in force an opposing feeling as soon as you are aware of what you have done.

You can use whatever props you need, in order to put you in mind of the thing you want. Use pictures, music, clothes and whatever else you would surround yourself with, once your dream has been fulfilled.

Always know that your strongest and most persistent feeling is the one which will be expressed. It is important to think in the positive present. You must say,' I *am* wealthy' and not, 'I *am going to be* wealthy as soon as...' Speak as though you are already in the state of the reception of your desire.

The feeling of 'I am' has prominence over the feeling of something you would like to be, sometime in the future. It is for this reason that it is so important to think in terms of what you are and never in terms of what you are not. Think in terms of the difference between hope and a confirmed request. The former may or may not arrive; the latter you know will be here. Follow these instructions and your dream will be fulfilled.

It is imperative that you are careful of your moods and your thoughts. The connection between these and your physical world is constant. You must know that your body and mind retain the remnants of your previous feelings and if not counteracted by an opposing mood, can result in disease. Only ever retain thoughts and feelings of despair, anger, depression etc., if you want these to manifest into disease and perceived bad luck.

In order to have your desires manifest, you must think of these desires with strong feeling and reflective feeling. In other words you must think in terms of your wish already having come true. Your desire can only be mirrored in your life in an exact copy of your mood. Therefore you must feel with faith, that your wish has already been received. It was granted as soon as you planted the seed in the domain of your subconscious.

Your subconscious does not judge whether your thoughts are right or wrong, or good or evil. It does not care, it is ambivalent. It plays the part of an android in your service. Whatever you are thinking of, it is going to provide, for you. That might be today or tomorrow, or two weeks next Tuesday. But it will provide and the sooner you become aware of your thoughts and feelings, the sooner you will see the thread which joins the two events. Then you will stop believing that fate, destiny, chaos or anything from the material world is creating the challenges for you. The point of your life is not to try and overcome whatever random and tough challenges are thrown in your direction 'in order to make you stronger'. It is you who is doing it to yourself. It is only you, who is bringing in every person who confirms the thought that you are only capable of doing this or that. It is you, who has projected the person who got that job instead of you, because you thought that you were unlucky or unqualified.

Apply to every situation the rule that you and your thoughts are the cause of your life. If you do this with an open mind, you will soon see that what I am telling you is true.

You cannot plant nettles and expect flowers to grow.

Test yourself, honestly. Keep a record and check it off. Look into your past and find connections between events. Do you say, 'I am always ill, poor, unlucky?' Were you ever determined to have a certain thing happen, regardless of what you were told, and it did? Perhaps you felt that illness could attack you at any point? And so it did. Another time you felt that you were well – and so you were.

When you review your past thoughts and actions, mentally change the outcome of those you do not like. Change those past thoughts and feelings through the states of mind explained in the following chapter. Imagine those results changed and don't accept the results you manifested previously. You are weeding out the restrictive from the progressive in your mind.

You are the one with all the power.

This recording and rewriting exercise can be enlightening and addictive.

Soon you will not need to do it quite so often, because thinking with awareness and planning will become your natural way of thinking. You will see that your feelings are indeed, what is shaping your world.

I am repeating myself now and offer no apology for so doing. Your subconscious will always express that which has been impressed upon it. As soon as an impression has been received, your subconscious begins working on the materialisation of it. Having accepted that this feeling exists within itself and is part of it, your subconscious must manifest an exact likeness of that feeling in the objective world. It will use whatever has been stored in your mind as habitual feelings and thoughts, however long ago that might have been.

It is your duty to yourself, to think only thoughts which you would like to see manifested in your life. And when feeling a specific wish, think of as many details of that wish as you can. Give your subconscious plenty to work with and it will not alter any details you have given it. It will only use events which match the feeling you are currently impressing your mind with and if necessary fill in the blanks with habit and memory.

Now, consider how many different moods you have during each day. It is a wonder anything stable is manifested. And the more you change your mind, the crazier your life becomes.

Choose what you want and stick to those thoughts of having received it.

Your mind will only accept and reproduce the feeling you are presenting it with. And for this reason, you must present it with the end result. You must be concerned only with your objective and never on how you are to arrive at that destination. In planning a path to your goal, you will naturally think of potential delays, problems, tactics and the rest. You are then informing your subconscious of the barriers it must present you with, in order to reach your destination. If you wish to arrive in Cornwall, safe and sound, think only of 'safe and sound' when you commence upon your journey. Do not think of road works, accidents, sick children etc. Set out joyously and imagining arriving safely.

At first, this way of going about your daily duties will seem difficult, but you will soon get the hang of it. Never try and not think of something you don't want to appear, once you realise that your mood has changed. Instead, accept that you are in a negative mood and then direct your mind to a better goal.

Your subconscious is the domain of your creation and will mirror whatever feeling and objective you are giving it. That is all.

You must also be aware that your subconscious is not your slave and so you must treat it as a friend who wants to please you. It will not and cannot alter anything you impress it with. It is you who must change your request. Your subconscious will happily drop what it is creating in order to begin work on the new and opposing object. But it will not produce it from subjugation, only love. Subjugation infers separation, love is inclusive.

Consciousness is one, and only divided between conscious and subconscious for ease of explanation and of creation.

You have to assume the belief and feeling that you will have, when you have been presented with your end result. The subconscious will only mirror and produce an exact likeness of your wish.

It is not enough to have a transient idea or hope. You must assume the feeling of the completed task and be happy for its materialisation. This is the only way that a wish will ever be manifested.

I know that it is easier to blame your current life in the sensory world. You have been taught that way. However, one day you will come to realise that your outside world experiences are only a mirror of what you have been feeling and creating in your subconscious. It is not the other way around.

It is not possible for you to see or experience anything other than what you have planted in your subconscious at one time or another. Your world experience is nothing more than your subjective thoughts, planted in your subconscious and objectively materialised in your outside world. You can only change your objective experiences by firstly changing your subjective feelings. Your subconscious will then change every detail in your objective world to match your subjective change. It will never change your objective world, without a change of feeling in the subjective. It accepts as true whatever you are feeling and creates only that.

You are the creator.

The only reason you cannot understand that you are currently what you want to be, is because you refuse to accept that you created it. If you don't like what is currently happening to you in your created objective world, then change your feelings. Think of what you want and know that as soon as you think it, you have already received it. You have to feel your desired objective from the point of view of the receiver. You will not reproduce the successful end result unless you think of what you want, from the position of what you are. You must live in the state of reception and must be conscious of who you are in the being or possessing of that state. Such as 'I am rich or I am well.'

You must deny the current evidence of your senses and feel what you would feel like, once you receive your desire. Pay no attention to the appearance that you don't have much money. Instead, pay attention to the sensory feelings that you imagine will apply when you are rich.

Are you getting it yet?

Once you master this awareness and self-control of your thoughts, it will be your highest achievement to date. From then on, you can be anything and have anything you want.

Initially it may prove difficult for you to learn, as you are going to have to use the mind which accepts the exact opposite of what I am telling you that you need to do in order to maintain self-control. But one day it will be your natural way of being.

A good way to start, is to reread these instructions over and over again. Hundreds and thousands of times if necessary.

When you practice on the small things, such as thinking of a person until they contact you, you will gain self-confidence. You can begin this very moment, no matter what you feel your problem is. Assume that you are well, right now and you will be just that. The speed of that end result will be in exact correlation to the faith you have in its truth.

In the following chapters, I will explain and describe how you can join with your subconscious and accelerate the process.

HOW TO USE SLEEP

One of the best ways to communicate directly with your subconscious is through your sleep. It is here that you can commune with your subconscious in it's natural state. You sleep away almost one third of your life and act as though it is only a way to rest from the tribulations of your life. But, sleep is the time when your subconscious merrily creates what you have been asking for all day. It follows your instructions to the letter, as we have already discussed. What you need to learn, is that the time prior to your falling asleep, is the very best time to think and feel your desires as you really want them to be. Then if you fall asleep in that mind, desired results will follow.

At pre sleep, you have moved mentally from your objective world participation and dropped right into the middle of your previously seemingly evasive, creator mind. During the time prior to falling asleep, you can discuss exactly what you want to transpire. Sleep will soon become a state you will actively seek out, once you discover the magical properties of becoming joined with your subconscious self.

Your subconscious has no desire of its own volition to change the objective world; it loves all that you have loved and love now. It will love the new world you request of it, with a similar passion. It will mould these wishes during your sleeping hours, while not being upset by your reactions to outside events. It will create these images in the exact likeness of your most consistent feelings and moods.

Fall into the state of having received your desire before you go to sleep. These objectified images will then present themselves to you during the two thirds of your life when you are not asleep. Nothing will prevent you realising your dreams, other than you firmly believing that you are not the person who possesses that thing, right now. Your subconscious will only give objective form to your wishes once you feel that your wish has already been granted. If your feeling is that, you hope it may arrive or you are going to receive it sometime, then that time can never arrive.

Tomorrow only arrives, once you believe it is today.

Everything manifests from within you and your self-conception determines what will appear in your life. This is the reason you must feel that your wishes have been granted prior to dropping off to sleep. Constantly adjust your mind and bring it back to your received mood, as many times as you must, before you fall asleep. You only manifest from within yourself the things you want; once you see yourself as the person who has the possession. You will never achieve possession if you believe you are the person who is still without and one day intends to be the person with. That is not good enough. You have to think of yourself as the person who has possession. What you are is what you perceive yourself to be.

When you become aware of incorrect self-perception, immediately change it.

To be clear, in order to make your desires real and objective, you must believe that you own, are or have witnessed your wish objectified. If you are confused about what that feeling should be, then close your eyes and imagine that you have your dream right now and how wonderful that would be. That is the feeling to take to sleep with you. Only go over the day's events in your mind, in order to change the outcome. Believe that you have altered any unhappy events from the day, during this process. And once you are asleep, the unsatisfactory outcomes can no longer interfere with your life. You may have to do this for many nights, but your work will reap rewards.

Your subconscious will work on the mood which it has been presented with for the night. Make sure that your mood is one of achieved positive growth and advancement. Your subconscious will not sleep, even when you do. The you that is you when you are awake, vanishes when you are asleep and your subconscious creates an alternate version of you to appear when you reawaken. It is through sleep that your conscious mind can join with your subconscious mind. There your subconscious creates in secret and reveals through your objective conscious mind, the person you believe that you are.

Don't worry if you do not get it right the first, or the fiftieth time. So long as you keep doing it, you must succeed.

Once you have made yourself comfortable in your bed, lying straight and on your back, close your eyes. If this position is uncomfortable for you, find a more comfortable one. But do remember, you are trying to stay awake for a little time, in order to get your sleeping mood correct. Do not try to stay awake. That has the same effect as trying to go to sleep; you will only succeed in remaining in the mood of trying.

Calm your mind and mentally run through your wishes and desires. Ignore what you may be experiencing to the contrary and imagine that your dreams have already come true. Take that feeling to sleep with you.

If you find it difficult to do this, because your mind is scampering away to your problems, just calm yourself and try again. You can create a fantasy that represents your desire completed. Walking arm in arm, with the wonderful person you want to be with, as an example. Eventually and perhaps quite soon, you will be able to perform this act more easily. Most importantly, never worry or keep thoughts of fear within you. Quietly and calmly fall asleep. Do this night after night, until your dream has been materialised.

Never forget that your subconscious only sees you as you perceive yourself and will faithfully produce events to match that belief. You are capable of changing your mood whenever you wish and herein lies the problem. Particularly while you are unaware. As a counteraction to these changing moods, you must pay no attention to the appearances and suppositions around you and feel only what you would feel with your end result at hand. This works just as well if you are despising the event you are hoping will not arrive. Or fearing it and don't want it to happen and it happens. You are thinking of a negative end result with strong feeling. Without an understanding of the process, you are then bemoaning that it is happening to you.

You should understand why now.

Acquisitions can only materialise following your mood and will not precede your moods. You become a different person following your change of mood and not preceding it. The mood change is an important key.

We are eternally dreaming our lives and yet our dreams are transient. These dreams would remain unreal, unless we assume the mood of their reality. Do not dream only of circumstances you feel that you could attain because of your past experiences, but dream of the highest dream you can desire.

Nothing is impossible. Nothing can be impossible if we are the ones creating our lives.

Think of that.

And if you can think of that, know that there are no limits. For if you can imagine a mood, then you can achieve it. You cannot imagine anything that is not achievable, or you would not be able to imagine it. Everything in this world was subjective before it became objective. It is your injecting the feeling of reality which brings results into the objective. You think of it and then imagine it is real. And it will become real. Your world will change with your conception of it.

This presents the wonderful realisation that the whole world and all it's inhabitants and events are only ever what you perceive them to be. You can alter your perception with every second and your perceived world will change in an exact mirroring of your new mood. These are experiences which I can only describe to you. But you must test the process for yourself.

You will be further convinced of the process once you have seen it in action. And if you were to believe it without experience, results will come more quickly. However, any practise or testing with faith and awareness will yield results quickly.

You do not tell another person of the part you wish him to play in your story either to his face or by letter or advertisement. You imagine what you want the other person to do or say and watch that event occur. You only have to convince yourself that he has changed and is now who you want him to be.

If you have some bad news, which you want above anything else to change, then change your mood within, until you firmly believe in a change. As soon as you have convinced yourself that your wish has been completed, then results must follow.

You know that you have successfully changed your belief in an outcome, when outside events alter.

If these events are not yet altering, go back into your mind and discover where you have failed to believe or adjust. There must be something, somewhere that you have missed, or changed results would appear.

Are you giving 100% to the process?

Ensure that prior to falling asleep, you feel happy and safe and secure. To not feel this, means that you are paying attention to the sensory facts of your life. Settle your mind and change your mood to the realisation of your granted wish. If the list is too long, or you are feeling particularly vulnerable, then do not go through and try and correct every problem you feel you have in your life. Choose a feeling or a picture that infers to you, that you are safe and secure and happy as a whole.

This does not necessarily mean that you should count your blessings. It means you should expand your mind to picture an ideal, probably not as yet experienced in your life. Pick a broad mood of happiness which infers that all is well. Then rest in that feeling, so that your subconscious can mirror your feeling for you.

Your days will gradually begin to reflect your change of mood and plan. The content of your days are filled with the mirrored effects of the causes you have planted in your subconscious. This is what free will means. Freedom of choice.

It is always pointless to travel through your day bemoaning other people's views and choices. Change your mood and your world changes. You can change every second of every day. You can change right this very second. The world will only change in it's relationship to you when you see it in your mind's eye as already having changed.

If you say all day, 'my boss always picks on me', he most certainly will. That is your fault and not his. He is an unwilling and unconscious player in your plan. Start thinking, 'my boss is always nice to me, he picks the best jobs for me', and watch the new boss appear. Remember that when you react to people and events during the day. You are also playing the part of the unwilling participant in someone else's fantasy.

Take control instead.

You can choose each day what you are going to accept. Or change. No one can do it for you. Events change, only when you change. When you unconsciously travel through your life, you are reacting without awareness to events you have previously planted in your mind. These have now been expressed and are magnified by your reactions. You make them truer.

This is why I say that you must pay no attention to the facts surrounding you right now. You are the mind that created them. All you have done, is forgotten the link between the two events. And once you pay attention to what you are thinking and doing, you will soon recognise this unbroken link.

And then once recognised, do not immerse yourself in regret for things done, or time unwisely spent. You are here right now, becoming aware of how to change.

Becoming awake to yourself is the most important goal a person can achieve. Anything is possible. There are no limits to what you can become. Imagine that you have already become the person you want to be and you will become that person. Feeling is what produces the state. The role you play in the world is dependent upon the perception you have of yourself. It is not your parents or your teacher or your partner or your boss.

All of this seems like a lot to take on board and then quietly go to sleep. But it isn't really. I have been repeating the same information in different ways for you to begin to understand. All of us hear the same thing over and over until one day a different word or picture, suddenly makes us completely aware of the truth.

And the truth is this.

As soon as you accept your end result (of which there will be many during your life time) and done it with feeling, it must materialise. If you do this prior to sleep and then fall asleep in this state of mind, then it must materialise.

When you wake, every action and event will mirror the state you fell asleep in, the dominant state. If this is not the state you wanted, then your power lies in reaction to anything which appears.

Choose the events to which you wish to react, the ones which fit your grand plan. This exercise falls into the category of paying no attention to unwanted facts. Today has been set out due to your mood of yesterday. It can be changed every second of every day, so long as you do not react and give further life to the unwanted events.

If you go to sleep with a jigsaw of emotions and beliefs and feelings which have gained momentum throughout your life, you will experience more of the same tomorrow. Each reaction creates yet another subconscious impression, similar to the event to which you have reacted. And then another action is objectified. There must be a powerful opposing and dominating feeling in order to contradict the future life of the unwanted events.

This is a powerful gift and it is only because you refuse to believe that you possess it, that your life does not follow the path you would wish. This gift can be used for good or ill and many who succeed have no knowledge of what they are actually doing in order to succeed.

This is your explanation of how you have real control of your life today and in the future, but are not aware of it.

While awake you can choose what it is that you wish to impress upon your subconscious. Then during your sleeping hours, the work is being done by your subconscious towards objectification. Sleep is the natural home of the subconscious and you are finding ways to communicate with it directly.

USE MEDITATION AS A DOOR

Meditation is similar to sleep in your quest for union with the subconscious. It is also possible to use the medium of prayer. Meditation and prayer can be interchangeable, so long as you are not praying to something or someone who is outside of you.

In meditation you are trying to mentally find the place between sleep and wakefulness. You are trying to find the space between your thoughts. The outside world and all of it's facts and reasoning are temporarily suppressed while you look for a blank canvas on which to write the next part of your life.

It is easier to impress your suggestions on the subconscious when your mind is quiet and receptive. Placing yourself in a sitting position helps you maintain the state for longer, as you are generally less likely to fall asleep during the process. Don't worry, it will not matter if you do, as we discussed in the previous chapter.

Breathe slowly and calmly and search for calm mental peace. Do not concentrate on the elimination of the outside world. Instead concentrate on the calm feeling. Doing this magnifies the effect you can have on your subconscious without distraction. You bring your desires to the centre of your mind and then confirm that your wishes have been granted and feel strongly that they have. All through your meditation you must acknowledge that you already have your dreams realised in order that this can become your truth.

The moment that you accept this fact, objectification commences. Meditation, like sleep, assists you greatly in this venture. Once you have gained self-control over your projections and intentions, you will perform all acts innately.

You will know that the only reality is your consciousness and that your thoughts and feelings are as real as any object or situation you may come across. You should never entertain any thoughts or feelings therefore, which do not make you happy. Whatever your happiness may be.

The person who finds this teaching difficult to accept, or the person who finds the teachings difficult to perform, are both victims of an uncontrolled mind. This person understands and accepts only the objective world and finds it almost impossible to shut out it's influence. This ruins any chance of furthering their skills by the use of their subconscious. They find it impossible to feel that their new wish has already been granted, because they believe more strongly in the sensory facts of the world. They think, 'I would love to have, to be..., but I cannot because of such and such.' This stops the positive creative process before it can begin. The mood is that of impossibility, set up only by their own beliefs.

No matter what they do, they cannot overcome their problems, because they cannot be anything other than they are.

Meditation is a state of mind where you can do the necessary mental work to change your mood and by definition your future.

I know that it is difficult when your senses are constantly informing you that you are not in possession of your wish. Your attempts to counteract this belief, by consciously repeating that you do in fact possess your wish, only seem to confirm that you do not.

Meditation helps you give in to the feeling of your desire and to do it calmly, rather than forcing your idea to materialise. If you think about it, you don't apply force to your mind, when you are creating your life normally. You just do it, without separating yourself from the act.

You cannot allow your feelings and negative emotions contradict what you are trying to achieve with your thoughts, because your feelings will always dominate the act. Your thoughts must be without effort, they must be calm and natural. You are trying to fix a state of mind, a mood and while maintaining self-control and awareness during your denial of senses, you must do it naturally and without effort.

It is achieved in this way.

In order to give in completely to your desire as a completed fact, you must go into your meditative state. There are many ways to learn how to meditate; some of you may already use meditation as a means to relax. But basically, you find a mental calm state, similar to the one you reach when nearly asleep, or nearly awake.

You are neither asleep nor are you ready to jump out of bed or off the couch. You are hovering somewhere in between. This is the place where you are joined to your subconscious without barriers. Here you can run through your desires and see them as finished, completed and in your possession. You do not run through how your wish was granted. That, you do not need to know or plan; you only need to feel that the wish is complete. This is the lovely quiet and powerful mental place that you will find yourself craving to return to. Being unaware of your sense world is a very comforting place to live. And it is here that you realise your dreams.

Even when you leave and return to your senses, the work is already underway to bring your dream into the objective world.

This is what I insist that you practice. You will soon learn that this is the way to your truth.

DAYDREAMS WORK TOO

Another tool in your chest is the trick of using daydreams in order to achieve your dreams.

When planning and wishing, you can place pictures in your mind's eye, in order to see what you want. Positively react to your dreams while you are there.

You don't know yet, but you use that same method to produce your current life. Turn these mind's eye pictures into a movie. See your terrible, boring, underpaid job as the fabulous job you want. Imagine your assistant sitting across from you, or the sales orders flying in.

If you want a partner, make believe that your single status is not true. Lay two plates at the table, put out two cups, imagine your friend sitting there with you. If you want to move, choose the house, the area and the furnishings. Make a scrapbook of the new décor and see it as yours, finished and done.

This is neither ridiculous nor pointless. Your dreams are being tightly focussed and connected to your habit loving subconscious, with this little tip. As you go about your day, pretend that you are already in your new job, house, or relationship.

You can pretend anything you want. You want a dog, so get a dog basket, food bowls and toys and put them in the kitchen and imagine what kind of dog you want in there. It will arrive, by perceived coincidence, contacts or some other, similar way.

Do not think that you are separate to any of your dreams. Do not think in terms of attracting your dreams. Those dreams are within you right now. You couldn't think of anything you cannot be or have. You cannot dream any dreams that are unattainable.

Absolutely anything and everything is possible. You only ever need to believe your wish is possible and feel that it has been granted and completed. You do not need to bring in a helper nor conjure up an enemy.

You can walk anywhere, if you believe you are safe. You can have anything, if you understand that the world is there for the taking. Once you have accepted the end result as true, you have removed your belief in problems along the way. If you still believe in problems, then you have not faithfully accepted the end result.

Which is it to be?

When you come out of your daydream, or meditation or slumber, know that you have set something in motion that can only be stopped if you react negatively when each step to the goal appears in your life.

It's up to you.

Realise that every dream or desire has a mood or state of mind that matches it.

Work out what the state of mind is that suits your desire and mentally put yourself in it. Then do not only believe in it, believe you are it.

No effort, no strain, no denial.

FURTHER ROUTES TO YOUR SUBCONSCIOUS

Sunbathing

There are many opportunities during your day and your life, to speak directly to your subconscious. While sunbathing, you don't always intend to sleep, often just choosing to relax and shut down your awareness of the sensory world. Now, sunbathe with awareness and daydream your wishes during your conjunction with your subconscious.

Bathing

Lying back in the bath is another opportunity. There is rarely an intention to sleep, only relax. You are now connected to your subconscious, speak to it there.

Running/Exercise

Often when running, there are many of those steps where your mind is saying stop, turn round, my legs hurt etc. Instead of listening to that negativity, use it as an opportunity to connect and daydream. Athletes often begin their event by visualising their successful end result. Remember to do this during your exercise too. Even if you are only imagining yourself riding around Aintree or winning the Tour de France, the practice is connecting you with the process of awareness in the creation of your successful life.

Sex

It is written in many places that sex is a way to join with your subconscious. However, although perhaps enjoyable, this process nevertheless generally involves another person. This means that you are separating your ability to connect with your own mind and furthering your belief that you need to do something with someone else in order to connect to your subconscious. That is not true.

Drugs and alcohol

For a similar reason to the above section, there is no need to involve something else, in order to create a bridge to your subconscious. Drugs and alcohol are really only altering your mind falsely and you believe that alteration to be your reality. I do not dispute that there have been successful experiments done where a healthy person has taken drugs such as LSD and experienced their own subconscious reality. But to set up a belief that your subconscious can only be reached by taking drugs has created a barrier for you, which can only result in problems.

Clairvoyants and psychics.

A clever psychic connects with their own subconscious quite easily and while in that state can connect with another's subconscious. They can tell what is likely to happen to that person, if they were to maintain their current mind-set. The future is neither random nor set in stone. It is possible to imagine many parallel worlds where a different version of you is living with a consequence of a decision you made. And you need to let go of that version of yourself and imagine yourself in a better world. The previous world, or state of mind, still exists, but you are no longer giving it life through your thoughts. This fact should be conveyed to the client and advice given on how to change their motivations. Then a different state of mind and subsequently future, is available to them.

Magic

If you analyse what is written throughout this book, the whole process can seem like magic. Abracadabra and you get all that you want. Although I agree that life is magical and once you truly realise that you are in control of life, you may well believe in the magic, the process is also scientific. In other words, you must perform certain practices in order to yield the results you want. These practices and results can be recorded and tested for verification. Some may call this magic and some may call it scientific and some may call it rubbish. If you call it rubbish, you aren't doing this with an open mind, are you?

FREQUENTLY ASKED QUESTIONS

I am often asked questions about this process and I hope by answering them here, perhaps more understanding can be gained by you.

Why should I believe this?

You shouldn't believe this without testing it first. I want you to prove it to yourself by following the given instructions and achieving results. Read this with an open mind and read it over and over again, until you understand everything I am telling you. Practice as I have described and soon you will begin to recognise the constant link between your subjective thoughts and your objective results. You will start to see an obvious connection and this will give you an incentive to try for further results. Soon this way of thinking will become part of your life. However, if you practice with the intention of proving this as bunkum, then bunkum will be your truth. You will have put up a barrier to your progression. Your determination to disprove the technique will in fact be proving the technique by disproving it. But you will be too blind to see. So, if you are going to try, be open to the prospect. Eventually you will learn to have faith, not blind faith, but faith with understanding. If you want to disprove it, then why are you here?

How long will it take to materialise my dreams?

That is a question to which we all want to know the answer. As soon as you accept the connection between your subconscious and the objectification of your wishes, you will want to know how quickly you can get your hands on the possession, or the state of mind. However, concentrating on time passing and the lack of your dream appearing, delays that very dream, in direct correlation to the thoughts you are projecting. All the time you are noticing your lack, you are not living in the successful end result. While waiting and worrying, you are mentally living in the sensory world which is currently confirming that you do not possess your end result.

The longer you notice lack and the more you worry about the non-arrival, you remain in the state of mind of waiting, of worrying. There you will stay, noticing the elusive desire until you change your thinking. You should be in the mood of reception, of noticing how much better your life is now that you have what you want. Your subconscious does not care whether your desires are good or bad, it is imperative to remember this. It will produce the illusion of waiting for your desire in the same way it will produce the reception of it. In other words, if you think you haven't got it yet, then you will always not have it yet. If you think you have it already, then your subconscious wants to mirror that event exactly and you will receive it. That is all the subconscious ever wants to do, to mirror your thoughts exactly. The whole story could be summed up with those words. Keep your mind focussed on the achieved goal and do not alter that belief. If you realise that your mind has moved, then swiftly bring it back to the receptive mood.

Will this help me deal with my illness?

Do not think in terms of illness. Think in terms of being well.

Will this make me wealthy?

You can only become wealthy if you believe you are already wealthy. Do not think that you must do this or that in order to become wealthy. Go into your subconscious as I have described and be wealthy. Then circumstances and events will arrive that will help you with this task. Those are the opportunities you will follow with enthusiasm.

How do I get rid of wrong thoughts?

Don't try. There lies a hard road and you will never arrive at your destination. Those thoughts exist in a different state of mind to the one you want to be in. Keep moving mentally to the new state and eventually the old thoughts and events will disappear. They live in the old state of mind and are waiting for you there, should you choose to return. There is no such thing as right or wrong thinking. There is only thinking. Your results will happen, because of your thoughts and beliefs and you should not be influenced by what someone else says that you should or shouldn't do.   I should point out here however, that you will have a far happier time if you choose good thoughts. That should be obvious to you.

Why are negative thoughts more powerful?

They are more powerful because you believe in them so strongly and your memory and habit has given them such force within you. You are so frightened when you feel those negative thoughts that they seem so real and immovable. That is all. Notice that fact and drop your shoulders and breathe more calmly, as you practice feeling happier thoughts. It is also possible to have negative thoughts without the fear feeling and those will result in an unpleasant story. Constant use of the methods we have described before, such as sleep and meditation, will gradually reduce the strength of those negative feelings.

How do I ignore the things I do not want?

Don't ignore them. The more you try and not think of something, the more you will think of it. If I say to you,' don't think of a horse,' what are you thinking of? And what colour is the horse? Accept that they are there for now and move your mind into the state of the finished dream. The practices we have been through, will gradually diminish the unwanted events.

Should I make changes in my life?

You should initially make changes in your thoughts, as we have gone over time and time again. Soon new circumstances will present themselves to you during the day. Merely throwing out your partner, for example, will not in itself help you, without a prior change of mind. However, as a result of the mood change, the first thing you may want to do is split. But that split you will feel comfortable with, having changed your mind first. You will then find it difficult to blame the partner or any outside events. You are aware that it was you who did it. You may have chosen to live in the mood of freedom, happiness and the desire to be treated well. Perhaps your partner did not fit this bill and you had a realisation that you needed to be single. If you want to give up smoking, just giving up is painful and likely to fail. But, if you live in the mood that you have already given up, then it will be far, far easier.

How do I change the past?

When you are connected to your subconscious through the medium of meditation or pre sleep you can bring to your mind an event you do not like. If you have received some communication that has upset you, perhaps you did not get the job, then mentally rewrite the news to suit you. If you have committed or experienced something which you find distasteful, then bring the event to mind and rewrite the result. Keep doing this until the new story feels natural to you. The effects from those events have been creeping into your daily life and affecting you when you did not realise. Past events have been affecting your current objectifications. I am telling you that rewriting that past event to have a more suitable ending, also affects your current life. And for the better. This same technique applies to anything, any subject, you are having trouble with.

What if I can't fall asleep or meditate?

Again, don't worry yourself about it. Practice the techniques of deep breathing and go to your mind and begin a story of what you want and feel as though you have received it. Don't concentrate on how long you have been awake; put your mind to what you want instead. Sleep will come soon enough. In fact, you are highly likely to discover that sleep arrives before you have finished your fantasy of your lovely new life.

How can I forgive my parents?

Forgive, forget, let go. How can keeping bad thoughts in your life help your future? You are constantly infecting your subconscious with these negative thoughts and so negative and similar effects must objectify yet again in your life. Move into the mood of forgiveness and security and live there for a while. Rewrite the events if you want. Eventually you will be able to let go. There is no point in allowing something that is in the past, continue to affect you today.

What happens when we die?

That question is a massive question and deserves a massive answer. But not one I can expand on here. What I will say is, we move from state of mind to state of mind for eternity. While unaware, we have no recollection of our past state of mind. Have a think about how that might apply to death and the state of mind that is death...

A SELECTION OF PUBLICATIONS

Of

PAGANUS PUBLISHING

Nirvana Moods and Dreams

Following on from **Nirvana**, A A Prideaux brings you a more detailed explanation of how you can use your imagination to bring about the life you want. If you have read **Nirvana** and want to study further and advance more quickly, then this book will help you do that.

Each chapter explains how you have been using your imagination to create many events you do not wish to experience.

You will learn that your whole world is created within your own imagination and then projected outside of yourself. You believe these ghosts are real and so react in ways which bring you more heartache.

Nirvana Moods and Dreams teaches you how to create sensibly and react carefully.

Shudder by A A Prideaux.

Who or what is Shudder?

The Old Mill was the place in Mill Town where most people worked. Years passed and the mill closed, but something remained inside. The townspeople had ignored the missing children and the frightening stories of devils and ghosts for as long as they could remember. It was easier to carry on and accept the money the Snooty family provided in return for working at the mill. Everyone allowed the Council members to run their lives and control their ideas without question. Questions were always ignored and the questioner punished. When Lydia Prix returned to the town after her marriage failed, she had no choice but to face the demons of the past and ultimately face the truth. The town would never be the same again.

If you go down to the woods today, you may end up being frightened of more than you think...

The Specials by A A Prideaux is a murder mystery set in 2012.

An old man is found dead in his home and DCI Revie and DS Jackson face the task of discovering who murdered him. At first, it appears that there is no reason the quiet widower should have been killed. But the investigation soon reveals that the gentle old man had been a long term and particularly deviant paedophile. As the story unfolds throughout the year and the body count rises, the police discover more people who have been living an apparently normal life while successfully hiding their past. The lives of all the people involved can never be the same again.

The Specials reaches its dramatic conclusion in Snowdonia.

A Ghost Story by A A Prideaux stars John Prideaux (1505-1568) lived in Stowford and had a wife and two children. He had lots of friends and great connections and lived in one of the largest houses in Stowford.

One evening in 1547, he and his family and friends were at their usual Tuesday night dinner. They took weekly turns as to which house the dinner and entertainment were held. This night was the turn of the Prideaux family at Stowford Manor. They ate their meal and as they settled down, John told the gathering a ghost story. He told them of a stranger he once befriended and the mysterious path the meeting led him along. Present at the dinner were Parson William Hele, Robert and Sybil Fox, Thomas and Joan Rogers and John and Ann Prideaux. Before the evening ended, the friends are on a mysterious quest of their own, leading to a remarkable conclusion at St Petrocs church on a snowy Dartmoor.

The story of 'The Bishop and the Witch' by A A Prideaux takes place between 1596 and 1608.John Prideaux was born near Dartmoor in 1578 and eventually became Bishop of Worcester. He spent most of his adult life at Exeter College, Oxford as Regius Professor and Vice Chancellor.

He was involved in many of the important events which took place in England during the reigns of Elizabeth I, James I and Charles I.

When John Prideaux gave evidence in 1606 at the Star Chamber about Anne Gunter, he did so as a well-known and respected Oxford academic.

At the 1604 Witch Trial at Abingdon her alleged tormentors, Elizabeth Gregory, Agnes and Mary Pepwell were ultimately found to be innocent. Anne was sent to stay with Henry Cotton, the Bishop of Salisbury until her father confronted the King and asked him to intervene in the bewitching case.

King James took a personal interest in Anne's troubles and put her under the control of Richard Bancroft, the Archbishop of Canterbury. Anne later confessed to King James that her symptoms were faked on the instructions of her father, Brian Gunter. He was arrested and faced his accusers at the Star Chamber in 1606. Anne Gunter was given a dowry by King James and she disappeared from the history books. History does not tell us what happened to Anne Gunter, but A A Prideaux provides us with a potential solution.

A A Prideaux tells the story of the possible meeting of John Prideaux and Anne Gunter at a much earlier time and how that meeting could have had a bearing on the outcome of the trial. Most of the characters playing a part in this story actually existed, making her version of events a possible one.

"John and Anne become friends and allies and we find that the story was not such a simple one. We discover who the real witches were and how John struggled with his faith during his involvement with the Gunter family. The reader must draw their own
conclusions whether the events were caused by demons or drugs.
This is an alternative tale based on historical facts and a lot of artistic license."

A A Prideaux

A Christmas Story by A A Prideaux is about Clifford Prideaux (1902-1963).The story begins in a modest home in early Edwardian Leeds, where the Prideaux family await a surprise event on Christmas Day 1902. The story takes the reader from 1902 to 1993 in a short story and gives a flavour of what Christmas meant to Clifford and his family. A Christmas Story gives a flavour of the times prior to the Great War for those with no money and no property. What the family had, was their love for each other and that love cannot be exaggerated.

A A Prideaux has written about each of her Prideaux ancestors from 1040 to the present day. She has traced every one of them through research and discovered where and how they lived. A A Prideaux has travelled miles in this search. She has old books, family documents and stories which have helped her in the conclusions drawn. Clifford Prideaux and her mother were responsible for setting the fire in her soul that turned into a Prideaux obsession. A Christmas Story is one of her fictionalised tales which draw on known facts. In this case, the story is written with personal experience of the author. This Clifford Prideaux (1902-1963) story takes us to Leeds and a tiny stone cottage full of love and warmth. These stories bring the Prideauxs to life, giving them personalities and allowing the reader to know them as people, not just names.

"A Christmas Story is about my grandma and grandad. Christmas was always a special time for Grandad Clifford. It's magic ran through his veins from the first day. Clifford was a kind man, but also a mystical one. Even after his death, he has visited his family on many occasions. I think of him as a hermit character, cloaked and walking with a long staff. He appeared in his role of Clifford for only 60 years before he returned to being the hermit." **A A Prideaux.**

Thank you. Do call again.

www.ingramcontent.com/pod-product-compliance
Lightning Source LLC
Chambersburg PA
CBHW020606030426
42337CB00013B/1242